TRIGGER
the
Wonder
Horse

An Inspirational Story of Faith, Healing, and Miracles

ANGELA LENHARDT

TRIGGER
the
Wonder
Horse

Lightin Up Media

Trigger the Wonder Horse
Published by Lighten Up Media
Denver, CO

Publisher's Cataloging-in-Publication data

Names: Lenhardt, Angela Dawn, author
Title: Trigger the wonder horse / Angela Lenhardt
Description: First trade paperback original edition. | Denver [Colorado] : Lighten Up Media, 2018.
Identifiers: ISBN 978-0-692-08330-7
Subjects: LCSH: Inspiration—Religious aspects—Christianity. | Christianity—Juvenile literature. | Horses—Behavior—Colorado—Anecdotes. | Horses—Diseases—Treatment—Popular works. | Horses—United States—Biography—Juvenile literature.
BISAC: YOUNG ADULT NONFICTION / Inspirational & Personal Growth.
Classification: LCC BR1-1725 2018 | DDC 248.8–dc22

QUANTITY PURCHASES: Schools, companies, professional groups, clubs, and other organizations may qualify for special terms when ordering quantities of this title. For information, email angeladlenhardt@gmail.com.

Lighten Up Media

For our beloved pets and furry friends. May you always be enveloped with unconditional love and a warm home from those who lay their hands on you.

Contents

Gratitude

I want to honor and give thanks for those who have given their time, money and energy in helping Trigger and I share this message with the world. You have believed in me, and for that, I'm eternally blessed.

To Dr. Page: Thank you for going above any human measure to keep Trigger standing on all fours and allowing him the freedom to live the best life any horse could ask for. He's a very lucky horse!

With deep appreciation for Bill Lancaster, Mark and Kate Urich and Scott Johnson for your generous support in publishing this book.

To Trigger's friends and the staff at the Equine Clinic: Thank you for going out of your way to be kind to him--offering an endless supply of cookies, carrots and hugs. And, allowing him to rummage through your cars, trucks and trailers because he thinks it's his "business."

To Trigger's fans: Words cannot begin to express how thankful we are for your love and support. Your prayers and well-wishes made the difference in this healing process. *WE* are forever grateful for *YOU*!

My Invitation

This book is meant to reveal how the power of love can heal beyond your wildest imagination.

In order to write this book, I had to experience it. Fully. Over the last seven years, I have consciously grown into the person I am today. At times, the journey has been painful, but it's also been rewarding.

What I've learned thus far is that God's guidance is clear and concise, and learning to follow the voice of the Divine isn't easy, but it's simple.

I've encountered numerous human teachers throughout my life, but none have brought me more love, joy and wisdom into knowing myself than my furry friends.

We're all created under the microscopic lens of Universal Intelligence, and it's time to bring into the human awareness that every creature counts and each one plays a significant role in the Divine matrix.

May this book inspire you to hug your pets a little bit tighter, and "see" them for the magnificent creatures they are. My hope is that children grow up knowing how powerful they are and choose to direct their energy in a positive and uplifting manner towards their pets, family and friends.

You are an extension of the Divine. May you know that you and your fur babies are watched over and blessed.

Namaste,

Angela

Anything is possible when you believe

CHAPTER ONE

In the Beginning

It was Halloween Eve, the weather was below freezing in Sedalia, Colorado, and the rain had turned into ice. Bailey, my beautiful buckskin quarter horse, had been in the corral and at some point during the night, had fallen and was unable to get up. The following morning, when I went out to feed him, I found him lying on his side, barely breathing. Bailey had developed colic (a painful obstruction in his abdomen) and it was necessary for him to be standing up again. I was all alone and encircled by hundreds of pine trees and scrub oak. The words "out-of-service" marked the screen on my cell phone, reminding me it was of no use, so I ran to the house to call the vet. I then sprinted to the neighbor's house looking for someone to help me pull Bailey up off the ground but had no success. I returned to the barn and Bailey was on his final breaths.

Helplessly, I lay on the ground next to him. We were both covered in mud from head to toe. All I could do was hold his head and pray that help came quickly. As I watched him take his last breath, the kind spirit that had once shone so brightly in Bailey's eyes softly disappeared, and he was gone.

Losing Bailey was a deeply traumatizing experience and I decided soon afterwards to get out of the horse business for good. I'd felt guilty, like I had let him down by not being a responsible owner.

I had purchased Bailey for one dollar from a cattle rancher, where it was either I take him home *today,* or he goes to the auction to be sold as "dog food." And considering he wasn't a horse for kids to safely ride—as his owner mentioned he had a "bucking" problem—I knew I was his only chance for survival. But my intuition and years of experience with horses told me his bucking issue wasn't because he was a "bad" horse who couldn't be trusted. Instead, I could feel he had experienced years of physical pain, and it was the person in command whose behavior was questionable.

A few days after I'd brought Bailey home, I arranged for a chiropractor to adjust the vertebrae in his lower spine, and then I diligently devoted time and energy into helping him unlearn his "behavioral issues." I *did* land on the ground a time or two as I paid the consequences for not knowing how to stay on and "ride the wave." Bailey never intentionally tried to hurt me; he'd stand patiently waiting until I'd catch my breath, then I'd hop back on and away we'd go. Fortunately, the training season devoted to breaking "old habits" through acts of positive reinforcement worked like a charm, because after a few weeks dedicated to trust-building, Bailey and I were a solid team.

Bailey was professionally trained by an "ol' cowboy" and participated in hundreds of "round ups" throughout his life. He chased cattle, working side-by-side with his furry friend, a border collie, who nipped at the heels of anything that moved. Bailey's movements were swift and deliberate. He could turn on a dime. After all, that is what his previous owner trained him to do. And breaking the habit of continuously having to "prove" himself and earn his keep was nearly impossible, as old conditioning is deeply ingrained within each of us.

One sunny afternoon while we were riding through the backwoods, Bailey saw a heifer that had gotten loose from its herd. From the moment Baily laid eyes on this wandering cow, the energy in his body instantly shifted, and his stance went from being relaxed to "let's move!" I held on for dear life. I came to full attention as soon as I noticed his ears perk up and his focus became intense. The power of his hindquarters transferred up through his spine, increasing his power of authority. He was ready to make a break and "head off" the loose cow as soon as I gave him my leg cue. Instead I assured Bailey by gently patting him on his neck and whispering, "Your old job is over, buddy." In the softness of my voice, he quieted down. Baily knew his permanent earthly "home" was with me—which wasn't long before he passed away.

Despite my decision to be done, God (or Spirit or The Universe, or whatever you choose to call the Source of Life) had another plan for me. Three days after Bailey's death, a friend of mine called and said, "Angela, a neighbor just told me about a horse nearby who needs to find a new home because he's being mistreated. But right now, neither one of us are in a position to do so and I thought of you, since you already have a stack of hay, a saddle and reins. Maybe you could help him out." I thought, *I have to do something for this innocent animal.* And in my heart I felt, *This may be an opportunity to make it up to Bailey, since I hadn't been "there" when he needed me the most.* Long story short, very quickly I'd found myself back in the horse business!

I rescued Trigger, a 14-year-old, light-colored palomino who stood 15 hands high, and he soon become my new horse companion. It didn't take long for us to build a heartfelt bond and deepen the connection of true friendship. Our foundation was based on mutual respect, leadership and trust. To begin with, I took him on long walks using a halter and lead rope, walking in front of him to define my "personal space" according to my path and speed. Once that was established, I led him by standing next to his shoulder and giving voice commands—walk, run, back, whoa—all while remaining by his side, learning how to be in sync with each other's cadence and rhythm. Eventually, I moved my way up to sitting on his back, cueing him through exerting pressure from my legs and/or a slight adjustment with the reins or the sound of my voice.

One Sunday afternoon early in our getting-to-know-each-other phase, I felt inspired to get some exercise, so I decided to enjoy the outdoors and spend time with my new friend. But because of my limited time-frame that particular day, I figured we should *both* walk, and I'd guide Trigger with a lead rope. My goal was to reach one of our favorite open spaces, next to a lake, not far from the barn, where Trigger could graze, and I could sit and relax. However, we faced a challenge. Getting to this particular site would require us to cross a busy gravel road and two lanes of highway traffic.

As it turned out we were able get across relatively easily, at least on the journey *out* to the open field, in spite of the traffic. When we arrived at our destination I found a place to sit and chill out, while slightly wrapping Trigger's lead around my wrist. Trigger began devouring the fresh green grass and I was soon relishing in mother nature's scenery and drifting into a peaceful, contemplative state. Apparently, though, I was *not* paying close enough attention to my surroundings— a deer suddenly leapt out of the bushes, startled Trigger, and he took off in a dead sprint for home. I jumped up and started running as fast as my legs would carry me but knew my chances of catching him were slim to none. Horrible thoughts of Trigger getting hit by a car flooded my mind as I chased after him —continuing to lose ground. I *knew* it would be practically impossible for him to cross the highway without causing a disaster!

As I raced down the trail in my vain attempt to catch up, I saw Trigger charge across the gravel road without hesitation. I thought my heart was going to thump out of my chest, while my mind was envisioning him being crushed by a fast-moving truck. I was wearing cowboy boots, which make it incredibility difficult to gain traction on the dirt terrain. I kept thinking, *How will I handle seeing him lying dead on the road?* Maybe I should just say goodbye now, I told myself. But my heart was saying something different. I intuitively heard, "I've got this. Stay focused. Trust me."

Amazingly, Trigger got across the gravel road okay. But then, he approached the faster, dangerous two-lane highway where cars and trucks were moving at a steady roar of 50 mph, without the ability to see what's around the bend. Sweat poured down my face as I reached a "dip" in the trail where I temporarily and completely lost visibility of Trigger—and in that moment, I was forced to trust that whatever happened was the way it was meant to be. My only hope was this: *If horses have angels, Trigger's will be paying attention and spare his life.*

When I came to the top of the trail, there stood Trigger next to a woman who I had never seen before—holding him by his halter. I couldn't believe my eyes.

Who is this woman and how did she get here? This was an unlikely road for anyone not on horseback. She graciously handed me Trigger's lead rope, and asked, "Have you lost someone?"

My words were limited to an out-of-breath thank you, expressing how incredibly grateful I was to her being at the "right place at the right time." But I had to ask, "How did you catch him? I mean, he was at a dead sprint for the barn."

She replied, "He seemed lost but knew where to go for help." I looked at Trigger. He was exhausted. His coat was drenched in sweat and his eyes were wide. Panic flooded the air but underneath the fear was Faith. There was a force dominating this situation that was much larger than anything I'd ever experienced. Trigger came to a complete stop for a woman whom he'd never encountered before. Imagine that! That in and of itself was a miracle. I couldn't believe what I was witnessing right before my own eyes. Approaching the woman, I felt weak in the knees, but her physical energy and emotions expressed, "It's okay."

I smiled at her, and Trigger and I headed for home. I had the sneaking suspicion that if I turned around, the woman would be gone. *And, I was right!* It was like she had vanished into thin air. I looked Trigger in the eye, and said, "You are one very lucky horse!"

Enjoying a roll in the snow

CHAPTER TWO

The Journey Continues

*I*n the early years of our time together, Trigger lived at the equine clinic just south of Denver, and absolutely loved it. This was also convenient for me because I lived within four miles of the stables. As I'd have to drive past the stable to and from my office, I could see him freely roam in the pasture, giving me peace of mind. The caretakers at the stables who were responsible for feeding him daily immediately fell in love with him, too. It was no secret that whoever was pulling a load of hay, carrying the feed bag or holding a handful of cookies was Trigger's "favorite person of the day," as Trigger would offer his appreciation through bellowing out a whinny to whoever spoke to his heart . . . or his belly!

In stature, Trigger has usually been the shortest horse roaming the pasture, but size hasn't seemed to matter to him. He believes in himself and his larger-than-life personality can be read by way of his facial expressions, which reveal exactly how he feels, moment-to-moment. When Trigger is happy and mellow, his eyes appear soft and his body language is relaxed. But any sensation of discomfort will be conveyed through the whites of his eyes becoming larger, a non-stop twitching motion of his ears, and his repeated stomping of the ground.

Generally speaking, Trigger is easy-going, mischievous and persistent. To this day, I wonder if Trigger has the skills to read, or maybe he's just got a great sense of smell. Who knows? But if he sees a sign written on the wall that says, "grain," he'll walk directly towards the bin and do his best to pry open any container, thrashing any barricade along the way. Seriously, if he ever has anything to be concerned about, it's the simple things, like how to display his pleasure or displeasure over a certain flake of hay or how to best invade another horse's space so he himself can stand in that one particularly good spot in the sun.

Yep, this horse has tactics for getting what he wants in life, and he's *very* direct. He'll make eye contact, lay his ears back, and make a beeline straight towards his goal. He's not intimidated easily, and he is typically adamant about "holding" his ground for what he believes in. I've seen countless times how this attitude has worked in his favor.

Trigger has also been the instigator of the herd. Whenever he felt the need to munch on various weeds, grasses and trees thriving beyond his living quarters, Trigger was for hire. He'd set himself and his buddies free by maneuvering a gate's latch with his mouth and then giving it a quick shove with his head. And once again, the caretakers would be hard at work wrangling the herd of four-legged critters back to the barn.

Weather has never been a concern for Trigger, and he seems to appreciate the difference in seasons. In the course of a year, he'll roll in the snow, dance in the rain, and lay in the sunshine. Truly, nothing fazes him. Many of my favorite memories have been when we'd participate in cattle drives, swim across rivers with me on his back, or enjoy the simple pleasures, like watching the sunset. Our relationship has been built on the sheer enjoyment of living life with deep appreciation and no expectations.

But the time came when I decided to sell my house and move into a "business arrangement" of owning ranch property with another individual. The price was right, and I thought having my own horse property would be nice—not realizing it was also a ton of hard labor! I relocated 35 miles southeast of where we'd been to an area called "the plains," because of how flat it was. Unfortunately after we'd made our move, I quickly recognized how unhappy Trigger was with his new home . . . and frankly, his feelings were mirroring mine.

I made this move without truly knowing exactly what our living conditions were like. Regardless of the fact that Trigger had a barn and other horses, the situation was uncomfortable, on every level. I had made a choice to move going against the "grain in my heart." Each time I drove onto the property, a lump would twist and turn, reminding me of my hasty and "bad" decision. Trigger knew it, too. He could feel my underlying angst because we were "one unit," and besides energy doesn't lie and neither does the inherent nature of an animal. Animals are born with instincts for a reason—to keep them safe; and if the owner is aware, an animal's behavior can also protect a human. Trigger's behavior would indicate exactly how I was internally feeling. If I was calm and peaceful, then he was a pleasure to ride. Conversely, when I was a "hot mess" then I'd better hold on tight because we were in for a rodeo.

The riding conditions on the property were horrible. The wind constantly blew, which makes riding more difficult and not as much fun. We were often forced to ride in barrow pits along stretches of country roads, trying to avoid the dirt and dust that was blown in our faces as farm trucks flew by. Also, broken fences and barbed wire were lying on the ground, plus there were holes everywhere—made by rabbits, ground squirrels and prairie dogs—forcing us to be constantly on the lookout, since holes in the ground can easily cause a horse to break a leg. Trigger also had to "fight" the other horses for food, and the people who co-owned the property didn't respect Trigger's space (let alone mine).

After a few long months of doing our best to adjust to our new situation, one windy afternoon, I felt guided to make an unexpected trip home to see Trigger. The woman who was entitled to the other half of our property had apparently taken it upon herself to ride Trigger without my permission. She had the reputation for using a "heavy hand" with animals, which I'd never personally witnessed but had heard about. Anyway, she decided to saddle him up without asking me. She had no idea I was there, and without making a peep, I sat quietly from afar, preparing for the "show-down"— knowing exactly how Trigger was going to react. In all honesty, he didn't care much for her much either, plus he didn't like anyone on his back other than me. But I knew he'd take care of himself in this type of situation. I actually felt as though I was waiting for an entertaining circus act to begin.

The woman jumped on Trigger's back and began flaunting her, "I'll show him who's boss" attitude, and gave him a swift jab to the ribs. Trigger's response was to walk backwards, refusing to follow her commands. He even tried to buck her off to prove his point. I snickered to myself when she got angry, but continued to sit, waiting patiently. Then she got off, and with a look of vengeance, smacked Trigger across the face as hard as she could. That's when I stepped into action. I jumped up, walked towards her at full speed, firmly planted my hand on her back, and said, "Can I help you with something?"

She handed me the reins and didn't speak a word. Within a few short hours, I arranged transportation from a friend who owns a horse trailer, and planned an immediate move for Trigger, and eventually one for myself. Trigger was off the property that day, and I moved shortly thereafter along with selling my half of the ranch.

At first, I wasn't sure where we'd be going, but my first concern was Trigger because I was confident in taking care of myself. I began to pray and picked up a local farmers' newspaper and began to look in the want ads. I saw the name of someone who was desperately seeking a calm-spirited companion for their horse, and I liked her vibe. I told her about our situation and without hesitation, Trigger was promptly welcomed into his new environment. This new location was ideal for him, as he had 40 acres of freedom to graze, adequate shelter and access to fresh water. The property also had the advantage of being in the middle of a neighborhood and surrounded by people of all ages. Ever since I'd owned Trigger, I'd seen that people adored him, especially young children. I'd watch as they'd put their hands through the fence to scratch his forehead or climb through the fence and groom his mane. Feeding him treats was also a highlight for everyone involved—his favorites being carrots and apples.

The only drawback was the drive for me, which was 90 minutes from the house I was renting. And unfortunately, there weren't enough hours in the day to visit him frequently, so our interactions were limited to once a week. I did my best to make this situation work, and we did so for seven years. But it was a long trek, particularly during the winter months when Mother Nature would dump snow and blowing wind would make the drive practically impossible. There were days when the roads were covered with a sheet of black ice. "Drive slow and keep your hands on the wheel," I told myself.

As time progressed, I started seeing "signs" that a change would be good for both of us. Trigger was officially becoming a senior citizen (in horse years) as he was 33 years old. Being an older horse, it was obvious to me that he'd require additional nutrition in order to maintain proper weight and a healthy fur coat that would keep him warm during the cold single-digits nights.

Using the wind to grow strong roots

CHAPTER THREE

The Winds of Change

*M*aking a conscious choice about our next location, I went online and Googled "horse stables" and found one nearby—eight miles from my house to be exact. I'd actually driven by it once—three years earlier—and recalled thinking, *Hmm...that place looks interesting!* The location was great, because it was in the center of a state park with all sorts of trails, rivers to cross, and plenty of horse buddies to keep Trigger company. In addition, he had his own stall and shelter, and the best part was the close proximity to my house, which made it relatively easy for me to see him daily.

We both loved this particular stable—long trail rides, leisurely walks, brisk runs, hours basking in the sun, and even a picnic or two—mainly just reveling in the elements of nature. And whenever I needed a solution to one of life's random questions such as: "Should I go on a date with this guy?" or "What's the best approach to this situation?" I'd put on my running shoes and take Trigger for a jog, side by side. We'd both be getting our exercise, but that's *also* when I'd receive my clearest insights into the solutions I was seeking—when we were both hoofin' it, and somehow I'd be most attuned to the inner guidance that steered me in the best direction.

But that "fun" only lasted a year, and soon life as we knew it began to change. It was early November, and a relatively cold month for Colorado. One day, I'd decided to leave my office early and venture out to the barn just to give Trigger extra love and attention. But when I arrived, I noticed my beloved friend had an odd-looking sore that had appeared overnight on the top of his right front hoof. Without thinking much about it, I figured he'd scraped himself on a piece of lumber and assumed it would heal on its own.

Unfortunately, that wasn't the case. The wound *didn't* heal. In fact, five days went by and it continued to get progressively worse.

Then I remembered Trigger occasionally stumbling on our runs. I hadn't thought much about this, until now. I had an overwhelming sense that something was frightfully wrong, so I called the veterinarian and set up a "barn-call" ASAP.

Because this was an emergency call, Trigger's primary vet, Dr. Barbara Page, wasn't available, so instead, she sent Dr. Jeff Kramer in her place.

When he arrived, Dr. Kramer took one look at the sore and said, "I think we need to take Trigger into the clinic for x-rays . . . today. How soon can you get him there?"

His diagnosis wasn't good. After a series of x-rays, the doctor could see Trigger had a growth that formed around the bones inside of his hoof and the internal sore had grown to be so large that it was surfacing. You see, before I took ownership of Trigger, his previous owner told me that he was in "little accident" with a barbed wire fence when he was a yearling. They didn't act concerned at the time, but the scar was evidence that it was more than "just a cut." Now, we were dealing with the remnant of an old injury 30-some years later. We had one option, and that was to surgically remove the obstruction so that Trigger would be pain-free and able to walk again. So, without question, I gave the vet the OK. Thankfully, I was hired the week before to speak at a women's conference, and coincidentally my compensation covered the cost of the procedure, almost to the penny, which was my indication that God was watching over us.

Dr. Kramer took charge of operating on Trigger's hoof that very afternoon. The surgery went as planned, although he *did* tell me Trigger's recovery would likely be a slow and arduous process because of the size of the mass he'd extracted. Still, he was confident Trigger would make a full recovery. What was ironic about this situation was the day that Trigger had his surgery, I was helping someone move, and accidentally dropped a 70-pound lamp on my foot! Ouch! So, *both* of our front "hoofs" were recovering. Talk about sympathy pains!

Anyway, Trigger was on the mend and free to go home a few days later. This was the beginning of our true test of faith.

Two days after the initial surgery, I made one of my routine visits to the barn. This particular afternoon happened to be quite frigid for Denver, and to my surprise, Trigger was lying down in his outdoor stall, showing little signs of movement. In fact, he had minimal energy to lift his head off the ground. His breath was shallow, his mouth was slightly open, and his eyes were mostly closed. I could see his spirit holding on for dear life. His fur coat had even turned a lighter shade of blonde. Instantly, my mind garnered the thoughts of my past experience of Bailey dying in my arms, and how there hadn't been anything I could do other than be "there" for him. I refused to accept *this* moment as Trigger's end. But ironically, here I was again, in a situation where I had to figure out a way to lift my horse off the ground if I wanted him to survive. *What is the life lesson?* I asked myself.

To complicate matters, there were three magpie birds lingering overhead with one sitting on his leg, pecking at the bandage, *trying to eat his hoof!* I was so angry at these black and white vultures swarming over Trigger's bloody hoof. Lucky for them I didn't own a BB gun! I chased them away with a demanding voice and tended to our business.

I did my best to be in a rational state of mind despite my panic. I knew this was a life-or-death situation and needed to get help fast. Without a horse trailer of my own, I felt helpless. I called the vet clinic in hysterics, and thankfully, Dr. Page answered. When I told her the situation she said, "I'll send help for him and you. Her name is Carolyn. She'll be there within the hour."

A huge sense of relief rushed over my body. But it was clear to me Trigger and I had some "work" to do before Carolyn arrived. At this point, Trigger was still lying on the ground, and it was totally up to me to get him on all fours, navigate his way out of a tiny gate, and move him to a location where Carolyn could back in the trailer, so he could be loaded.

Getting him upright was the first step, but there was another major factor involved: the time of day. The sun was setting and there weren't any barn lights available to shine upon the safest route. Between my being alone, the stress of the tasks at hand, and the looming fear of death, I began losing hope that Trigger would survive.

The terrain at the barn was a complete mess. It'd been raining for days, huge potholes were everywhere, and the chances of Carolyn getting her truck and trailer stuck were highly likely. I started praying that she had the skills to carefully back the trailer down the narrow path, squeeze between two buildings and the corral, and avoid the bigger holes so the trailer didn't sink. I had no idea how this goal was to be accomplished considering the circumstances, but tracing back to our previous life's experiences, I knew better than to distrust the power of the Divine. I was forced to trust that Trigger's angels were listening and able to help us to take one step at a time with utter faith and patience.

I put my hands underneath Trigger's body on the ground and began to push him up. With all of my strength, I said, "Trigger, you have to believe in yourself. Right now. I know you're in a lot of pain, but you have *got* to get up!" As I continued to lift, I kept encouraging and reminded myself all I need is a mustard seed of faith to move mountains....I prayed.

Take one more step

CHAPTER FOUR

Believe in Yourself

Over the next 20 minutes, Trigger did his best and mustered up the courage to stand, even though he winced with each move. Finally, he was up and firmly standing on three legs, because the fourth, injured one was essentially of no use. I wrapped a halter around his head and proceeded to guide him forward, one step after another, mindfully and slowly to the gate. The pain on his face was heart-breaking for me to witness, and I wanted nothing more than to "fix" him. But I knew that this process was in God's hands and I needed to remain calm, persistent and just do what I could: stay focused on getting him loaded into the trailer.

Each step was excruciating for both of us. Many times I wanted to cry, but I also needed to be strong for my best friend. He trusted and depended on me, and I knew that if he sensed my internal self-doubt, that would hinder our ability to succeed. As we were edging our way to the spot where he needed to be, we gracefully maneuvered our way down the path that was covered with rocks, loose gravel and holes dug by varmints. To help him remain steady, I put my left hand on his withers and my right hand on his hindquarters. My primary concern was to avoid the holes, so that he wouldn't get his hoof stuck . . . but if he *did* fall, I would be in the position to catch him on his way down.

As darkness fell except for the shimmering essence of the moon, my greatest fear had come true. Halfway to the loading pad, Trigger stepped into a hole with his "good" front hoof and 900 pounds came crashing into me like a ton of bricks. His weight pushed me back into a pile of old two-by-fours, but I was prepared, both mentally and physically. With an intense sense of commitment, I focused my energy into catching him mid-air and set him back onto his hooves.

I was cold. Fear tends to do that, but the temperature had also dropped about 20 degrees. With adrenaline pumping through my entire body, I looked directly into his eyes, and said, "Alright, we need to make it over there," and I pointed in the direction towards the landing pad. "Keep going!" And Trigger obliged!

We were almost to the loading area when I *finally*

heard the sound of a diesel truck roaring down the single lane road. It was one of the best sounds I'd heard in years. I turned my head and saw headlights on the way to our rescue.

When Carolyn arrived, she stepped out her truck and I instantly felt she was "heaven-sent." From the brown coveralls, flannel shirt, leather gloves and her precise steering ability, I was confident that I could trust her. I didn't have any time to analyze the situation more than that. Carolyn could see we were in a serious predicament and time was *not* in our favor. As she expertly maneuvered the trailer back between a shed and old irrigation ditch she turned on every light on the truck and trailer, which gave us the opportunity to properly see. The truck and trailer were practically glowing, it was so bright!

Finally, Trigger and I made it to the foot of the trailer, but we still had to address our next, unexpected obstacle. The trailer didn't have a ramp; therefore, Trigger was going to have to step up about two feet to get in. For a healthy horse, this would hardly be an issue, but that wasn't our situation, and this distance felt as though we were about to climb Mt. Everest.

As I stepped into the trailer, I was wishing he'd naturally follow me, but he must have been thinking, "I don't think so," as he came to a screeching halt—and it didn't appear he was going to take another step. My hands started sweating, my heart was pounding and both fear and doubt began screaming in my mind.

I remained focused and proceeded forward, gently tugging on the lead rope and pleading, "*C'mon*, Trigger. I *know* you can do it!"

But he wouldn't budge, and I ran out of patience. I anxiously began pulling, yanking, and jerking on the lead rope, whatever it was going to take. I was trying to force him to load, and in response he braced himself to the ground with his three good legs. There we were, pulling in opposite directions when, without any indication as to why, Trigger began placing his sore foot onto the trailer and gradually sliding it backwards, over and over again. It was like he was calculating how much pressure his injured foot could actually support. And even *more*, it appeared he was taking the dimensions of the horse trailer. He smelled from side to side, then lowered his head, smelling from the dirt on the ground to the floor board, as if he was measuring the width and height of the space. Suddenly, he put both legs up, but then immediately backed down.

I was growing more and more tense with each passing moment, and shouted, "C'mon Trigger! Get up here!" I couldn't deny how I was feeling. My shoulders were so tightly wound that my ears were practically resting on them, and I felt as if my stomach had been struck with a wrecking ball. I was almost out of energy—but determined not to quit. Unfortunately, my words conveyed the energy of fear—and Trigger emotionally and physically felt it.

Without hesitation, Trigger looked at me, turned around, and headed in the opposite direction. He was exhausted and stressed out, and it was evident Trigger wasn't following me anywhere.

And in that precise moment, I knew *I* was the problem.

I asked Carolyn, "Have you ever seen a horse in this amount of pain load into a trailer?"

"Yes, I have."

"Do you believe Trigger can do this?"

"Yes, I do."

"Then I will step down so you can take the lead."

Carolyn jumped in the trailer and called, "Okay, Trigger, you can do this, buddy."

And in one breath—it was as if he'd sprouted wings and gracefully lifted himself up—Trigger was inside the trailer. *I'd never seen him move so fast.* Within *five seconds*, Trigger was loaded, and we were headed down the highway.

When we arrived at the clinic, it was 7:30 pm and the weather was freezing. Dr. Page was there to greet us, and once again, Carolyn took charge and unloaded Trigger. Unloading was almost as much of a challenge as loading, but he navigated his way like a champ.

"Baby steps backwards," I kept saying. I was reminded of watching a child play hopscotch. Trigger would hop backwards on his hind legs, and then slide his front hoofs underneath him.

When he got to the ledge, Carolyn said, "Step down now." He clearly understood her commands because in a flash, Trigger was unloaded with all fours on the ground. Dr. Page's vet assistants put Trigger in the barn and carefully began attending to his medical needs, and Dr. Page sent me home.

With nothing to do but practice being patient

CHAPTER FIVE

Looking for Hope

*O*ver the next few days, it was challenging to remain hopeful in a situation where the future was uncertain. Knowing there wasn't anything I could physically do to alter Trigger's condition, I sat in stillness. My alarm went off in the early morning and I rolled over to sit at the end of the bed. This was one of the darkest moments in my life, literally. My best friend wasn't feeling well, and no amount of sympathy could change the way Trigger's situation. It had been days since I opened the window shades. I could say that I was even falling into a state of depression. I was trying to remain positive, but with all things considered, the financial costs of veterinarian bills and Trigger's age, the future seemed grim. In that moment, I felt angry, sad and fearful, and I realized that I'd stopped taking care of myself with the simple things, like eating and exercising for my own well-being. And then the Divine interceded and began to speak to me.

God: Are you going to open the curtains this morning?

Me: Nope. I'm going to choose to sit in the dark.

God: Are you sure?

Me: Yes.

No doubt, this conversation ended abruptly because I had to get into the shower and begin my day. I had obligations to see clients and calling to cancel is generally something I don't do—plus, being around others assisted me in keeping my mind off of my personal issues . . . even as what I dearly love, his health and mine, was quickly dwindling.

When I returned home that evening, I walked into the house, ready to head straight to bed.

Every light was turned on full-blast and beaming towards the middle of the room. It was like I was standing in the center of a runway, and I know I didn't leave one light on when I'd left that morning. In fact, I was sure of it!

Me: (In my best grumpy voice) Really? What is this about?

God: I thought I would add light on your situation.

You can do this

CHAPTER SIX

——

Making Room for Healing

Although Trigger was receiving the best medical care possible with round-the-clock supervision and hourly doses of medication, he was resistant to eating or drinking. That posed a problem, because with all things considered, proper nutrition was certainly a necessary ingredient for maintaining his strength and healing regimen.

Minutes began turning into hours, then a few days had gone by, and Trigger still hadn't touched an ounce of hay or drunk any water—fortunately, he was intravenously getting fluids, but this was only a temporary solution to a bigger problem.

As time would permit, I spent every free moment with Trigger. Late one morning, visiting Trigger at the hospital, I was standing next to my beloved friend when Dr. Page came to have a heart-to-heart conversation with me. She said, "We'll have to make a decision about Trigger's future soon, if he isn't willing to eat or drink."

I looked at her and understood what she was saying but couldn't fathom the idea of Trigger being euthanized. In fact, the idea brought tears to my eyes and the sobs were unstoppable. I couldn't imagine not having my best friend by my side, and my heartache increased when reflecting on all we'd been through over the years. He'd been the one constant figure in my life, my veritable support system: spiritually, emotionally and even physically. Struggling through my mother's death, my divorce, relationships, the death of my dogs and cats, and transitioning through various homes and businesses, Trigger had been my "rock" for over 20 years. But I refused to make him suffer. His quality of life was in the forefront of my mind; and if and when I decided to euthanize him, I wouldn't wait until *I* was ready. I'd do it when the time felt right in my heart and allow him to "go home."

For example, I'd make the decision if I were to see Trigger experiencing an immense amount of pain, which would be mirrored in the depth of his eyes . . . because once his eyes stopped shining and became dull and heavy, it would indicate he was truly weary of his condition. Another scenario would be if Trigger was spending more time lying down than standing up, because it would represent that standing on all four legs was too agonizing for him to bear. And certainly, I felt I owed him respect for his level of pain and how he felt, as well as whatever dignity and grace could be afforded to him at the end of his life, unlike watching Bailey make his final transition under extreme pain and duress.

Calmly, I laid my forehead against his and said, "There isn't anything I want more for you than to heal, but I can't do this for you. You will *have* to connect to that part of yourself that knows what to do." Saying this to Trigger broke my heart. But I wanted to empower him like I would anyone else on their journey. And what if my energy was so closely tied to his healing process that in some way, I was prohibiting it, and my lesson was to detach and experience the Miraculous?

With nothing more to say and feeling emotionally depleted, I left the clinic and went home to sleep.

I drove away knowing this situation was now out of my hands, I'd done everything I could, and it was now time to wait and see what the future held . . . and to pray.

As I was driving back to my house, I remembered some of the best advice that I'd ever been given: "Let go and let God." These words inspired me—once again—to release my "need" to control the situation;

and instead allow God to be in charge and direct life accordingly. Micro-managing situations isn't my area of expertise, anyway. I figure that's why I hire professionals and ask God for guidance while understanding that the "test" can be in the waiting—and the energy I behold while patiently "waiting" for Divine instructions.

I felt myself relax into a state of grace, despite the circumstances, and when I got home, I went straight to bed and drifted off to sleep.

The next morning, I woke up to the sound of my phone ringing. It was Dr. Page telling me Trigger had miraculously eaten every morsel of his grain *and* drunk two buckets of water during the night.

"Thank you, thank you, thank you!" were the only words I could speak. "Thank you, God. Thank you, Dr. Page, and thank you, Trigger, for rallying with heart and soul!"

God was on the move.

With each passing day, Trigger seemed to gradually improve. And the more I hung out at the stables, the more I realized how life is to be lived—in the present moment. I pondered questions such as: *How can I devote more love to this situation that it can positively influence the outcome?* and became very observant of Mother Nature. *If God created this universe—there isn't anything He can't do.* I needed to keep the faith.

Trigger was now eating, drinking, lying in the sun,

taking naps, and maintaining his strength and muscle tone by meandering from one stack of hay to the next. Although I knew he was in a tremendous amount of pain, whenever I saw him, his ears perked up and his eyes would shine. I took these behaviors as a "sign" we were likely on the best possible path for his healing. Still, I understood that if his behavior should change for the worse, then other decisions would have to be addressed.

But until then, Trigger's "hello" whinny and shiny eyes were enough for me.

The intense monitoring Trigger needed for his recovery required him to temporarily live at the clinic, and this fact eventually became financially overwhelming. Soon, I didn't see how I would be able to keep up with the expenses, but I remained committed to keeping my faith and praying for guidance.

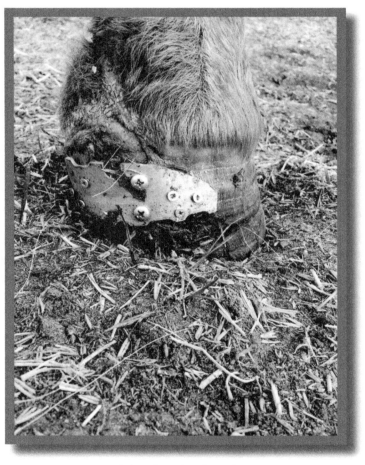

A hoof made of steel

CHAPTER SEVEN

―――

Home Free...Almost

Trigger's hoof frequently needed "special" shoes. These consisted of a mold that allowed the bones in his foot "room" to move, along with proper fitting of a metal plate and screws placed strategically across the top of his hoof to keep it intact and prevent the hoof from entirely cracking into the coronary band. This was a financial worry—properly fitted shoes are expensive but necessary, and God placed a farrier in our path who understood the proper mechanics for properly aligning Trigger's hoof.

At this point, it seemed Trigger's healing was progressing with only an occasional abscess and infection to handle. But at least, I wasn't spending every waking moment wondering if "this is the end." I had hope...

It wasn't long before the clinic's entire staff, clients, and fellow horse patients fell in love with this four-legged fur ball. So much so, that Trigger's rehabilitation extended to the luxury of allowing him to freely roam the entire property. Trigger got to go wherever he wanted, whenever he wanted and however he wanted!

Trust me, this horse *loved* the fact that he could wander in and out of the barn as he pleased. But because he wasn't officially a "boarder," he couldn't be in the pasture with the other horses. So, he had to settle with visiting them from the opposite side of the fence. Depending on his mood, Trigger seemed to take pleasure exercising with the geldings as he'd prance up and down the fence line despite his pain, wearing a fashionable boot made out of duct tape preventing any moisture to re-infect the injured area. Besides, Trigger has an ego. It's kept him alive for 36 years. He was determined not to allow the other horses "see" his less than perfect strut. Head held high, tail arched, and a dramatic whinny demonstrated his willful attitude and determination to succeed. And when he wasn't showing off, he'd be in the barn peeking around the corner, or hovering over Dr. Page's shoulder to carefully observe the other patients or their treatment protocol.

Eventually, Trigger found himself a "job." Whenever a sick horse would arrive at the hospital, he would offer his support and inspiration by standing next to the ill patient and "holding space" for his furry friend to heal. The veterinarian assistants called him "The Helper."

Trigger's temporary housing status only lasted approximately two months. It was interesting because I'd been praying that *maybe* Trigger could have found his forever-home on this property. I wasn't sure how that could be arranged though since Trigger was quite a bit older, and weaker than the rest of the herd. But one day, Dr. Page graciously said to me, "Trigger has found himself a home 'here' if you're interested in boarding at the clinic, and we'll make it work for him."

My heart exploded with joy. I knew this clinic was the ideal place for him, because he was surrounded by people who loved and cared for him, he had plenty of horse buddies, and a surplus of carrots and "horse cookies" to keep him happy. But what was even *more* intriguing about Dr. Page's proposal? It seemed life had come full circle. Trigger had lived at this exact equine clinic 14+ (yes, same clinic) years prior, and lo and behold, The Universe guided us to become residents on the same property again! Our journey appeared to be coming "full circle"—even to the extent of him living in the exact same pasture when we he first arrived years ago.

Trigger was steadily gaining strength; his mobility was increasing, and he continued to heal. However, he *still* wasn't living in "close quarters" with the other boarded horses. He had his own stall at night, and freely walked around the property each day. His foot was only 50 percent healthy, and neither Dr. Page nor I desired to run the risk of him being re-injured by being kicked by the other horses. Being the "new kid on the block" determines the pecking order when integrating with the herd.

Until he'd recovered a bit more, and put on a few extra pounds, his daily regimen remained the same: he was only permitted to visit his "friends" from a distance and then taken into the barn at night for shelter.

But Trigger is persistent. And one day he was determined to live with his friends, the mares. To him, that's where he belonged; and since horses are herd animals, many typically prefer to live within their animal comfort zone.

So, one day, Trigger pulled a fast one on the caretakers. As they were taking in a fresh load of hay for the "girls," Trigger snuck in behind the tractor and propped himself in the middle of them—and that's where he decided to stay, *with his girlfriends*. I couldn't catch him if I tried!

Generally speaking, Trigger was fortunate, in this regard. The mares were somewhat nice, meaning they didn't run him off or deliberately hurt him, although it naturally takes time for the hierarchy to be re-established whenever a new horse enters the domain. And since Trigger was the "low man" on the totem pole, being older and healing from an injury, he knew to play it wise and stay out of their way. But he didn't seem mind—he was just happy to have found his place.

At the same time, the expenses continued to accumulate. It seemed there was always another medical procedure required to drain the infection, another round of antibiotics, pain meds, bandage changes or custom-made horse shoes. It got to the point where I felt like I'd sent him to college and back, twice, within the same year! And the truth was, I knew we'd never be able to enjoy another trail ride together, but that wasn't his primary role in my life, nor was performing in arenas or winning blue ribbons. He was my loyal friend. The deeper issue remained whether he'd ever be able to walk again without daily medical treatments from Dr. Page or her staff.

Because I devoted every additional penny to Trigger's healing, I no longer had discretionary income to spend on anything "extra." My family and friends soon began to take it upon themselves to call and offer their "two cents" of advice on what I should do about "our" situation, which didn't go over well with me. At one point, someone whom I considered a good friend unconsciously spouted off the remark, "Don't put any more money towards that old horse. What's the point?"

I responded, "If you don't believe in me or my horse,

and you're not offering encouraging words of support, don't bother calling," and I hung up the phone.

But then, the seeds of other people's doubts began to take root in my mind. I began ruminating about what they'd said, and I started losing faith that Trigger could gather enough strength to fully recover. It only seemed like common sense to be logical and make *that* tough decision in choosing to end his life.

I spent many hours in prayer and meditation asking God what I should do, as well as asking myself the important questions, such as: "What are my priorities? What brings me the most joy? What else would I be doing with the money if I weren't spending it on Trigger?" My answers came quite clearly. Trigger was my priority, and he was my responsibility, and he brought consistent joy to my life . . . *every single day*. And for me, that was priceless. Sure, I could've devoted my discretionary income traveling to Bali, buying a new car or finding a bigger place to live, but was that what I really wanted? Fortunately, I deeply connected with my heart, and eventually came to my "horse sense."

Despite Trigger's situation and rhetoric from family and friends who didn't truly understand why I was driven to do what I needed to do, there was a pull operating within my heart that wouldn't allow me to give up without exhausting every alternative. "Hold on one more day," I repeatedly said to myself.

I decided to keep working toward Trigger's healing, and began to pray and ask God, "Will you give a sign on how I can continue to afford these vet costs?" The spiritual message I received came through loud and clear. "You know what to do. Teach classes on what you've learned about helping others heal."

It's funny to me how bold, yet how straightforward this "reply" was. I've been doing this sort of intuitive healing work for 16 years. I had the credentials and helped hundreds of people over the years through one-to-one intuitive sessions and group workshops, so this decision felt "right" as it was in alignment with who I am. So, I said, "Okay God. I'll do it," and began my preparation. Within a short amount of time, I organized the necessary information, put a structure together to convey the material, and announced the workshop to my email list; and within 24 hours, the class was entirely booked.

As I collected the course fees from the class participants, once again, God answered my prayers as I was only a few dollars short of paying off Trigger's total bill. *Amazing!* Again, this was just the confirmation I needed to remind myself we were *still* on the right path.

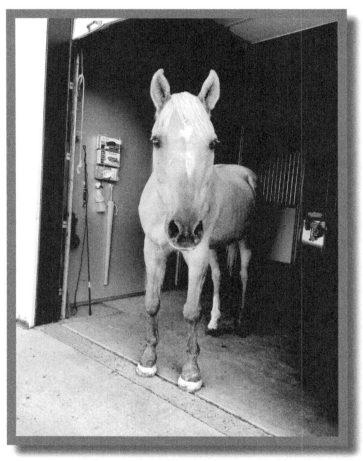

Sportin' brand new shoes. Air Trigger!

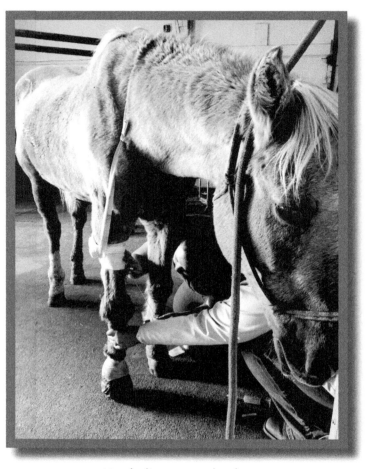

Not feeling so good today

CHAPTER EIGHT

Cultivating Our Miracle

I didn't miss a day visiting my furry friend and maintaining an optimistic outlook that everything was going well. After all, it had been a month since our last "scare" of him needing an emergency treatment due to another infection.

Another month went by…

And then…

Unbeknownst to Dr. Page, the vet staff or me, a debilitating abscess was growing in the bottom of Trigger's front right hoof, again! He was fine one day and lame the next with no explanation. There was no visible evidence of infection or an obvious cause of his pain. But apparently, the bones in his foot were rubbing against each other, creating friction and inflammation, which called for another invasive procedure. UGHHH!

This semi-emergency happened on a day Dr. Page was out of the office, so the "on-call" doctor took over. However, I'd been alerted and given my approval to go ahead and do what needed to be done, and then immediately drove over to the clinic. Just as I pulled into the parking lot, Trigger was lethargically walking out of the barn with a bandage five times the size of his hoof. I was *devastated*. Having to watch Trigger be put through another medical procedure I was forced to ask myself if I was acting in his best interest, or was I doing this for me? Why was his healing process so difficult!? As I walked into the barn to speak with the doctor, the sight resembled a war zone: blood, bandages, gauze and syringes were strewn everywhere, and the strong smell of manure filled the air (because every time Trigger underwent a procedure, he'd get sick to his stomach and diarrhea would be covering the floor or splattered on the wall). Wanting to get the doctor's opinion of how she felt about this procedure, I also decided to ask her opinion about the entirely of Trigger's "situation."

With a caring tone, she said, "Things don't look good. He's working against the odds and his age isn't making things any easier." I leaned against the door. My eyes began to shed tears. My stomach was tied in knots as she continued, "Let's have Dr. Page check him again tomorrow. She's the expert." I knew that before I jumped to any conclusions, it was in everyone's best interest if I stayed centered, and not allow my emotions to get carried away in controlling my actions.

I agreed, thanked her and got into my car, but a flood of tears erupted from my eyes. My heart ached, and I sobbed for I don't know how long. When I stopped, I wiped my face with my shirt sleeve, closed my eyes and said, "God, what should I do now?"

I intuitively heard: "Go to the church, get holy water and pour it down the length of his spine."

Without hesitation, I followed these instructions like a school kid.

I realized I needed a container to collect the holy water, and the only place I could think of that might have one was the grocery store. When I walked in, I headed to the salad bar and grabbed two small plastic holders with lids (typically used for salad dressing) and then I drove to the church.

I entered and sat in one of the pews. I'd spent countless hours communing with God in this particular church following my mother's death. Between the burning incense and the sound of the baptismal fountain, the ambiance gave me a sense of serenity. Many times throughout my life, there'd been moments when I found myself having "down" time in between client appointments and felt compelled to sit in the devotional cove which lined the walls with hundreds of lit candles. Today, I felt I needed the healing as much as Trigger did. By putting myself in an environment that knowingly promotes spiritual, mental and physical well-being, I figured this part of the equation was needed for a successful recovery. I've often heard the saying, "What is within one is within the whole." In essence, the healing that I needed for my own peace of mind could only benefit Trigger's situation since we're all connected through the threads of our hearts. I continued to sit in the pew for a few minutes longer, and began asking God, the angels, my mom, friends, whoever would listen, that if they could hear me to please give Trigger another miracle. After I felt my prayers were complete, I mindfully (and gratefully) got up from the pew, dipped my containers into the water basin and headed back to the stables/veterinary clinic.

Not seeing Trigger standing in his "regular" spot, I ventured out to the pasture. He saw me coming and stood peacefully until I made physical contact with him. I held the sacred water with great respect. I knew that if I wanted a miracle to "show up," then it was required that I set the intention to surround us with healing energy and light, internally and externally, and remove all doubt from my mind— and trust God was omnipresent.

I held both containers of holy water up to Trigger's nose, and he sniffed, showing he was curious about what I was carrying. All of a sudden he took a deep breath and dropped his head into a submissive position.

I looked at him and said, "Trigger. This is going to help you heal," as I poured the contents along the center of his back. He took another long, deep breath, his eyes softened, and I saw relaxation move through his body. The sensation he experienced was palpable to me.

I repeated the Lord's Prayer ("Our Father...") a few times, as I purposefully began visualizing a divine light moving through the palm of my hands, permeating through Trigger's body and infusing positive healing energy into his hoof. When I was finished, I gave him a kiss on his forehead and said, "No matter what happens, it will be okay. Trust." And then I left. But as I was walking away, I was compelled to turn around. I stared at Trigger for a moment; I couldn't deny the holy water had formed the sign of a cross down the leg of the injured hoof.

Pray without ceasing. I knew God was in our corner.

The following morning, Trigger was Dr. Page's first patient. She had heard about the stressful events of the previous day, so after her assessment, she called me right away. Not knowing what I had done, she said, "Why are you so worried, honey? This horse is walking around just fine!"

I smiled, along with another sigh of relief washing over my body. "Thank you, God. Thank you, God," I said as I hung up the phone.

I felt as though we were on track again and

remaining optimistic.

But after this last medical procedure, the costs of Trigger's medicals bills weren't appearing to cease. And again, I was forced to have another one-on-one conversation with myself about my priorities and how to keep "things" in perspective. In order to help me sort out the details in determining Trigger's future, I arranged for a personal appointment with Dr. Page, so she and I could discuss the physical and financial consequences if his foot continued to weaken. Our meeting was arranged for Wednesday morning of the following week.

I need a big hug

CHAPTER NINE

Love Heals

The Sunday before Dr. Page and I met for our appointment was a beautiful day. I devoted the entire afternoon to sharing time with Trigger. I was reading, and he was grazing. It was a perfect day—80 degrees and not a cloud in the sky. I was truly hoping we'd overcome the toughest part of this journey, and I was looking forward to hearing good news for once. Even those who boarded their horses on the property were commenting how wonderful his recovery had been and they could verifiably see a "kick" in his step.

That day couldn't have gone any better.

On Wednesday morning, as I was driving to my office before I met with Dr. Page, my phone rang. It was one of Trigger's favorite human friends, who made contact with Trigger each morning to give him his breakfast. But that day she called to tell me Trigger was lying down in the pasture and couldn't get up.

My heart sank. I immediately took the nearest exit and raced like an Indy driver out to the clinic, canceling my client appointments as I drove.

Knowing I was already on Dr. Page's schedule, I began wondering, *Is this meant to be? Is today the day I put Trigger down?*

Mentally, I'd been preparing for this day over the course of the years; after all, Trigger was 35 years old and had been through severe trauma, and I knew he couldn't live forever. So, I prayed for the courage to make the best decision in Trigger's highest and best interest. But when I arrived at the clinic, he was standing up in the pasture. Hardly moving, I'll admit, but at least he was upright!

I crawled through the gate and entered the pasture. Trigger didn't whinny his usual "hello," and his head was hanging slightly. I took deep breaths as I approached him, and then wrapped my arms around his head and gave him a big hug. I put a lead rope around his neck, hoping he'd want to follow me out of the gate and into the open space. If at all possible, I desired to feed him at least one more batch of his favorite mixture of grains before I'd have to make that *last* dreaded decision.

He made the effort to walk with me, although it

took 30 minutes for him to move 30 feet. We took our time, we were in no rush. I poured the grain into his bucket and as he began to eat, I decided to make a quick trip to the coffee shop and return to await my appointment with Dr. Page to hear what she had to say about Trigger's future.

When I returned with coffee in hand, I'd noticed that Trigger had walked himself over to the area where they euthanize the horses. It's a space on the ground where the renderer can easily pick up their bodies and take them to be buried. It appeared Trigger knew what he was doing. My heart immediately sank deeper than I ever imagined it could, and I truly thought, "This is it. I'm losing my best friend today."

All the physical evidence pointed in the direction that Trigger was no longer meant for this world. I sat next him and began to cry. This wasn't the first time I'd been forced to make this heart-wrenching decision, but Trigger was at that time the only animal presence on this earth who'd brought me such an immense amount of joy, comfort and peace . . . and I ached knowing those things were going to be taken away within the hour.

Hannah, one of the vet assistants, came to sit with us. She loved Trigger as well, and we began to talk about how he'd already overcome so much, but now, this was probably the best for him, considering the circumstances.

As I was sitting next to Trigger's head while he was lying on the ground, I could tell he was listening to every word as his ears were twitching with each syllable coming from my mouth. Maybe it was time that I came to grips with reality and accepted the way "it" appeared to be. It was time to face the truth. I quietly leaned over and gazed into his eyes. With tears streaming down my face, I said, "Trigger, are you ready to go and meet God?"

Like a lightning bolt, Trigger stood up. The expression on his face was, "What! No way! I'm not ready yet!" He couldn't run away fast enough from me. And he made a beeline to the nearest hay stack. Unbelievable! It was as if he was saying, "Look, mom! My life isn't over yet...I still love to eat!"

Hannah and I stared at each other with astonishment. Neither of us could believe our eyes. I simply said, "I guess not." And the truth is, I didn't know whether I should laugh or cry. Apparently, Hannah was thinking the same thing, as a stunned look was plastered on her face as well.

"I'll get Dr. Page," Hannah said as she walked away and headed into the clinic.

That morning was another busy one for Dr. Page. She was tending to an emergency situation that came in around the same time Trigger decided to lay down. But when she was finished with her patient she came rushing out to evaluate Trigger's seemingly hopeless situation. It appeared that she was also a bit taken back by Trigger's behavior of lying down in the place where horses are typically euthanized, but remained confident and said, "I have a game plan. We are going to do one more surgical procedure to Trigger's foot to remove the infection, and possibly the bone. I've already arranged another vet to assist me. He'll be here within the hour." The infection was overwhelming his body and affecting his ability to stand—we didn't have a lot of time to consider any other possibilities.

Dr. Page knew exactly what needed to be done. Listening to her, without wanting to make any hasty decisions based in doubt, I was silent. The emotions rushing through my body were intense: a combination of happiness, sadness, excitement and fear. I didn't know if "this" would be the surgery that worked, but I had to at least give it one more try. Especially because Trigger was willing to live. He'd proved it. But then the "common sense" button kicked in again. I suddenly blurted out, "How much will this cost?"

Dr. Page replied, "We are doing this surgery, Angela." Her tone of voice didn't offer room for me to disagree. "You and Trigger have a big job in this world, and if people want to help you, then let them." I nodded my head okay. I didn't want to ask for help. I didn't want to show my weakness, but if this was my only option to keep Trigger alive, then I needed to "suck it up" and humble myself in order to turn this situation around.

I thought, *I'll mention to the "prayer warriors" on my Facebook page that Trigger is having another surgery,* as I've witnessed personally, when two or more people join forces in prayer, miracles happen. And it only seemed like the natural thing to do since I'd been sharing pictures of Trigger, inspirational memes and status updates since 2007. So, the morning of his "last" surgery, I posted, "If anyone feels compelled to offer prayers, love, positive mojo or support of any kind during this time of uncertainly, I'd be eternally grateful."

I drove away from the clinic. I needed space to breathe and take my energy away from interfering with his surgery and found myself sitting in a coffee shop drinking multiple pots of green tea. Dr. Page told me she'd call when the surgery was over. Hours went by before my phone rang. It was Dr. Page: "Trigger is doing great, and he's already walking around." Granted a generous amount of pain killers were moving through his bloodstream, but the fact that he was alive, and mobile, was a positive sign.

Then the voice of reason began creeping in again. This surgery was going to financially set me back another year, or maybe even two!! *Who cares?!* I pushed back against my thoughts. I made a conscious choice to do what I needed to do, and I chose Trigger over money, and I was willing to pay the consequences. Whatever it was going to take, I was willing to pay off my debt for my loyal friend.

By the end of the day, the office assistant called to share more words of good news. She said that Trigger had a generous outpouring of support from friends, family and Trigger's "fan club" who wanted to contribute to his life-saving procedure. I was blown away. Total strangers called to say that they had seen Trigger's face as they scrolled through their Facebook feed, and mentioned that his face inspired them to continue another day. The donations came close to the cost of the surgery! I was speechless. Knowing that God works through all of us in various ways was affirmation that I'd made the "right" choice. We were given the opportunity to appreciate the lesson of learning how to fully receive and give. The outreach of support from *so* many generous and kind-hearted people, many of whom I'd never met, was truly humbling. So much love, encouragement and support had been extended to me and my horse—WAY beyond my wildest dreams—and I thanked God for each blessing and for placing loving people in the center of our lives.

Love heals

When life gets you down, look up

CHAPTER TEN

Life Lessons Learned

I've discovered allowing more light, joy and laughter into your heart will reflect your greatest gifts. In addition to sharing this story, our mission—Trigger's and mine—is to reciprocate the kindness that was extended to us during times of uncertainty by making guest appearances in senior centers and schools. But I can't decide who has more fun, Trigger, the audience members, or me. My heart overflows with joy each moment we walk into the front doors and witness the various facial expressions of those present.

It's no secret that Trigger loves children, and his tolerance level is beyond any human I've ever met. Trigger has been known to play the age-old game of "hide and go seek." One day during his recovery the electrician came to the stable to finish a project and brought his four-year-old daughter. The young girl's father un-strapped her from her car seat and let her run freely without knowing that Trigger was also on the loose. The moment the little girl noticed Trigger, she ran over to him, and began to hug his leg, jumping up and down, but Trigger stood still. He even turned around and nuzzled the top of her head. There are photos to prove it! She then proceeded to chase Trigger around trees and through the barn. He was busy trying to escape her, but then he'd peek around the corner to see where she was. Their game continued for 20 minutes or so, until her father was finally finished with his work and then discovered what his daughter was up to. Needless to say, Trigger is an excellent "sitter."

I've received multiple Divine blessings from the time I've spent with Trigger, many more than I could ever count or possibly describe in words. But if there is one golden nugget of wisdom that will forever be imprinted in my mind is that, *YOU HAVE TO BELIEVE IN YOURSELF, AND TRUST.*

I understand that the vast majority of people haven't been given the opportunity to develop a relationship with a horse like Trigger, let alone witness the wondrous, unexplainable miracles we have. But in relating my first-hand experiences, I want everyone to know cultivating your own miracle through harnessing the power of healing *exists within your heart;* and is for all of us to experience when you undoubtedly *trust* in the process of the Divine.

Perhaps, we're always in the presence of our spiritual teachers, especially when we're noticing our own reflection in the mirror—for instance: recognizing a behavioral trait in an animal or a certain characteristic in another human being that may resemble our deepest emotions. Pay attention. What underlying "tone" is expressing itself through the face staring back at you? Fear? Abandonment? Joy? Love? Rejection? This awareness is an opportunity to examine your own deeply seated truths, and in that way gain insight into healing aspects of your life. Their behavior is pointing you in the direction of where to examine your own roots. There are many indications why a human attracts a particular animal if you're willing to see beyond the rational mind. It's almost as if the Divine is placing an opportunity in your hands in owning an animal so that you can "work" on and heal aspects of yourself—through recognizing what is being mirrored back at you on a deeper emotional level. Owning any animal requires responsibility, dedication and time, just as it's your responsibility to devote responsibility, dedication and time to heal suppressed wounds within your own life.

Horses are prey animals and their survival depends upon a hierarchy demonstrating strong leadership, which is also the duty of a responsible owner. Horses require adequate time, energy, money, and frequently change "hands" between owners before the end of their lives. In the beginning, it may be difficult to build rapport with a horse, but compassion and patience are a must, as horses are generally willing to trust when they feel as though they've landed in a safe place.

When I first experienced the grief of Bailey's death and told myself "I am done with the horse business!" it took God to show me how narrow my own mind had become. And in order for me to expand and realize my highest potential, I was forced to surrender my limited perspective and discipline myself to hear Divine wisdom. But isn't that how life naturally unfolds, anyway? Based upon my direct experiences, when I was willing to release the tight grip on the reins of life (pun intended) and make room for God to lead, life opened doors into greater abundance.

As of today, Trigger's life continues to inspire many as he no longer needs surgeries, custom-made shoes, bandages or medications. His favorite thing to do now is to kick up his heels when a storm is brewing and chase his buddies around the pasture. He also has the reputation for rummaging through open car doors, the back of trucks, and walking into vacant horse trailers looking for a something to eat. Trigger's hoof has taken almost two years to fully recover. Granted, Trigger received excellent medical care, but the energy that seemed to carry him through his struggles was generated by the power of prayer and love extended to him from kind and generous-hearted people that continue to surround him daily.

Riding on Trigger's back is definitely an activity of the past. But that has never been my priority in our relationship, anyway. Sharing time with him has always been a soulful, sacred experience for me; and there's no way to explain the joy I've found just sitting with him alone out in the open fields or walking with him among the herd of horses, with whom he's now been a "family member" for years.

If there's one thing I know for sure, it is that when the Universe opens the door for an opportunity to learn, grow or be of service to another human or animal, take it. This may be the "test" in seeking the miracle you've been waiting for. It isn't *if* you get "bucked off" in life, it's *when*, but be courageous and get back in the saddle—and carry on. Every experience is a stepping stone into a greater awareness of knowing who you are while trusting you're moving in the right direction amidst the face of uncertainly. God's Grace and plan is gently revealed in divine time, and nothing surpasses the power of prayer, an open mind and a willing heart.

And if you ever need guidance about anything, let alone a ton of it, just say "yes" to asking the Divine to intervene, as the voice of Wisdom holds the key for a miracle to manifest at anytime or anyplace. Trust. You never know when it'll show up, in the most unexpected place or from the most unexpected stranger . . . just like it did for me and Trigger the Wonder Horse.

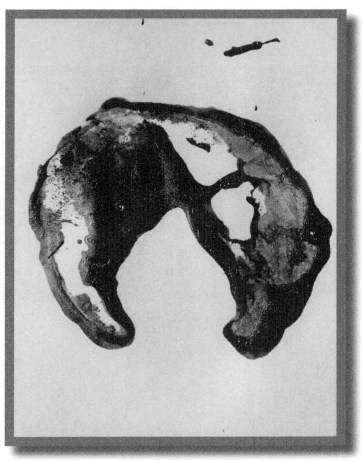

Trigger the Wonder Horse
"A magical hoof"

Angela Lenhardt

About the Author

*A*ngela Lenhardt, author of the best-selling memoir *A Charmed Journey: An Inspired Guide to Personal Transformation*, is an intuitive life and business consultant and spiritual teacher. She has been sought out by celebrities, entrepreneurs, CEOs, and hiring managers for her intuitive and healing abilities. Angela enjoys working with individuals and organizations of all kinds around the country. She utilizes her intuitive gifts to provide her clients with clarity on how to successfully maneuver through obstacles and guidance on how to avoid future pitfalls that may directly impact their lives.

Angela works with her clients in one-on-one consultations via phone or Skype, as well as in group settings at workshops, healing events, and retreats. She owns a private healing center in Denver, Colorado. For more information about Angela, see her website AngelaLenhardt.com, and for more information on Trigger, go to TriggerTheWonderHorse.com.

Made in the USA
Monee, IL
18 June 2023